Primary Science for Teaching Assistants

Also available:

Primary Mathematics for Teaching Assistants
Sylvia Edwards
1–84312–428–9

Primary ICT for Teaching Assistants
John Galloway
1–84312–446–7

ICT for Teaching Assistants
John Galloway
1–84312–203–0

Primary Science for Teaching Assistants

Rosemary Feasey

Routledge
Taylor & Francis Group

LONDON AND NEW YORK

First published 2007
by Routledge
2 Park Square, Milton Park, Abingdon OX14 4RN

Simultaneously published in the USA and Canada
by Routledge
270 Madison Avenue, New York, NY 10016

Routledge is an imprint of the Taylor & Francis Group, an informa business

Typeset in Bliss and Celeste by
RefineCatch Limited, Bungay, Suffolk
Printed and bound in Great Britain by
Bell & Bain Ltd, Glasgow

British Library Cataloguing in Publication Data
A catalogue record for this book is available from the British Library.

Library of Congress Cataloging in Publication Data
A catalog record for this book has been applied for.

ISBN10 1–84312–447–5 (pbk)

ISBN13 978–1–84312–447–4 (pbk)

Contents

v

Acknowledgements

I am indebted to the many teaching assistants and teachers who I have met during in-service sessions who have talked to me about supporting science teaching and learning. I would especially like to thank Kay Coverdale, Advanced Skills Teacher, for offering material and advice.

My heartfelt and sincere thanks go to my good friends Roy and Anne Phipps who once again so kindly agreed to read through the draft manuscript of yet another book and offered suggestions with such grace and patience.

This book is dedicated to my cousin Christine Smith, a brilliant teaching assistant, whose advice on being a teaching assistant supporting science has been invaluable. Thanks Chris!

Introduction

This book on supporting science is aimed at teaching assistants but I am confident that it will be welcomed by all involved in teaching children science, including teachers and those training to teach.

Teaching assistants are now an integral and important human resource in schools. Over the past few years they have assumed greater responsibilities, having been encouraged to support children and teachers across the curriculum. Many teaching assistants are comfortable supporting children in literacy and mathematics and these are skills that need to be transferred to supporting children in science lessons.

Science, however, offers challenges for teaching assistants that are different from other curriculum subjects, ranging from a new set of skills and subject knowledge to approaches that are to some extent unique to science, for example, the use of concept cartoons or specialist equipment such as magnets and Newton meters.

This book takes the reader, step by step, through issues and strategies relating to supporting the teacher and children in science lessons. Each chapter begins by setting out the key issues to be developed and finishes with a summary that reminds the reader of key points from the chapter. This book encourages the reader to reflect on their own experiences and understanding in science by engaging in short activities. The reader could carry these out as individuals or with other teaching assistants or in discussion with their class teacher. Personal reflection is an important part of professional development and this book is aimed at the professional development of the reader, whatever their level of experience.

While the book is aimed at those working with children of primary age, staff in secondary schools may find it a valuable resource for helping those pupils who require additional support in science.

Primary science is a wonderful subject, full of surprises, awesome experiences, challenges and excitement. I hope that this book helps you to enjoy bringing science to life with young people.

CHAPTER 1

What is primary science?

In this chapter we will explore:

- why science is an important subject in the curriculum;
- how scientists think and work;
- how children think and work scientifically.

Why science is an important subject in the curriculum

Have you ever thought about why science is in the school curriculum? Did you like science at school? Do you have any science qualifications? What do you think of scientists? Do you know anyone who is a scientist? The aim of this chapter is to encourage you to reflect on your understanding of science in relation to your role of supporting science in the classroom.

What do children think of scientists?

Look at the picture of a child's image of a scientist. Where do you think children get their ideas about scientists from?

Figure 1.1 How a child might picture 'a scientist'

Children develop their concept of the 'eccentric male scientist' from media such as comic books, films and television. But rather than have children think of 'mad scientists', it would be better if they thought of scientists as people from everyday life, such as doctors, nurses, engineers, pharmacists, electricians, aunties, uncles. It would be even better if, when they drew a picture of a scientist, they drew a picture of themselves! Science education aims to develop children's understanding that science is all around them and that people who engage in science come from all walks of life.

Why should children be taught science?

Why do you think science is such an important subject in the school curriculum?

SOMETHING TO THINK ABOUT

Jot down your ideas about why science is an important part of the school curriculum.

Science is an important part of the curriculum for many reasons:

- to help children understand the world they live in;
- to encourage children to be curious about their world;
- to help children appreciate how awesome the world is;
- to engage and use children's natural interest in and curiosity of the world around them;
- to develop the potential of those children who are interested in science to become the scientists, technicians, doctors, pharmacists, nurses of the future.

Most importantly, we teach science at school so as to develop a future generation that has some understanding of the key ideas in science and the way scientists work and can apply scientific knowledge and skills. We expect children to be literate and numerate; we should also expect them to be scientifically literate.

We should expect children to be able to make sense of scientific information so that they will be able to make appropriate and informed decisions as adults. Those decisions might relate to:

- personal health;
- public health, such as the risk of catching bird flu or mad cow disease;
- supporting environmental groups;
- engaging in a science based hobby such as gardening, astronomy;
- just enjoying making sense of the world around them;
- helping their children with their science school work!

Science and everyday life

Science is such an important part of everyday life. Your doctor uses his or her scientific knowledge to make a diagnosis; an electrician makes sure your house is safe; you know that bleach needs to be kept away from children because it is dangerous.

Scientists work every day to extend human knowledge of the world, developing new medicines, materials and even food. Just think, without science we would not have some of the following:

- frozen food
- aeroplanes
- mobile phones
- insulin.

FROZEN FOOD

Clarence Birdseye was born in 1886 in Brooklyn, New York, and invented a way to freeze food and deliver it to the public.

AEROPLANES

The American Wright brothers flew the world's first powered aeroplane, on 17 December 1903.

MOBILE PHONES

Dr Martin Cooper is considered the inventor of the first mobile phone. Cooper made the first call on a portable cell phone in April 1973.

INSULIN

In 1922, the Canadian physiologists Fred Banting and Charles Best discovered insulin.

Science is essential to everyday life and it is therefore important that children develop their understanding of the world and of how scientists work.

How scientists think and work

Let's consider what scientists do and how they think. Here are some of the things they have to think about and do when they are engaged in their work.

What scientists think about

- What to research, questions to ask
- How to answer a question
- How to set up an experiment
- What they will do
- What equipment they will need
- How to make sure it is a fair test
- What information they might need
- Who they might need to help them
- What they think will happen
- What to measure
- How accurate they need to be
- How to record their results
- What conclusions should they draw
- Reflecting on and evaluating their work

What scientists do

- Find someone to work with
- Talk to other people
- Make decisions
- Try things out
- Choose equipment
- Take measurements
- Write their results in a table
- Draw a graph
- Clear away
- Talk about what they did
- Tell other people about their work
- Go on the internet to find information
- Read books to find information
- Use a computer

How children think and work scientifically

> Look at the lists of what scientists have to think about and do. Have you seen children 'think like a scientist' or 'do things like a scientist' when you have been working with them? Jot down your ideas about this.

You have probably seen children do most of the things scientists do, which means that they can think and work like scientists. Primary science is based on how scientists work. It focuses on developing children's ability to think and work like scientists. It demands that teachers provide opportunities for children to engage in activities that are designed to help them:

- take an interest in science;
- think scientifically;
- develop scientific subject knowledge;
- work scientifically.

Taking an interest in science is about developing positive attitudes and awe and wonder in science. Thinking scientifically is about developing an ability to think like scientists – asking questions, finding ways to answer questions and solve problems, looking at information and evidence that has been collected and making decisions and drawing conclusions. Developing scientific subject knowledge is about develop an understanding of different concepts in science such as: forces, electricity, magnetism, changes in materials, plant growth, the human body. Working scientifically is about developing the ability to observe scientific phenomena, explore, carry out activities to answer scientific questions and solve problems.

The role of the teacher and the teaching assistant is to develop children's ability to think and work scientifically and to enjoy their science.

Think about your own experience of science as you were growing up. What was it like at your primary school and when you went to secondary school did the way you were taught science change? How? What kind of things did you do? Was it your favourite subject or was it your worst? Do you like science or does it frighten you? What do you think makes a successful science lesson?

All of these questions are useful to ask as they are aimed at helping you develop your understanding of what makes a good science lesson and what motivates children to learn in science. When you have been working with children, why do you think they have enjoyed science lessons?

SOMETHING TO THINK ABOUT

Read the comments in Figure 1.2 (see p. 8) made by teaching assistants about their own science education. Which comments best match your own experience?

Whatever your experience of science is, you will probably have some idea about how to make it a positive learning experience for children.

SOMETHING TO THINK ABOUT

What makes a good science lesson? Make a list of those things that you think help to make a lesson successful.

A successful lesson is many things:

- fun
- exciting
- interesting
- relevant
- hands on
- linked to everyday things
- accessible

Figure 1.2 What some teaching assistants have said about their experience of science lessons

- engaging
- motivating
- challenging
- respectful of ideas and contributions.

And a good science lesson teaches science knowledge and develops science skills.

How can the teaching assistant support primary science?

The role of the teaching assistant in science is to develop his or her own understanding of the science being taught in the classroom and work as part of a team to help develop children's understanding and ability in this curriculum area. The following chapters aim to help teaching assistants develop their ability to support teachers and children in science lessons.

REMEMBER

- Primary science aims to develop children's ability to think and work like scientists.

- Science is important to everyday life.

- Science lessons should be fun.

CHAPTER 2

Lesson planning

In this chapter we will explore:

- schemes of work;
- lesson plans.

Schemes of work

Like all subject lessons in the curriculum, those in science need to be planned. In this chapter we will look at the kind of documentation the teacher uses in science and in lesson planning. It is important to remember that all schools are different, so there are differences in the way teachers plan, organise and teach science. However, there are some basic elements that are common to all schools. Understanding these will help you in your role.

All schools should have a set of documentation that teachers use to ensure that science teaching is linked to science in the National Curriculum and the individual school policy.

The National Curriculum

Each United Kingdom country has its own national curriculum for science, which sets out what and how science should be taught, as do many other countries worldwide. Schools are expected to use this as the foundation for science teaching and learning. Most national curricula for science divide science into two main parts, first scientific knowledge and understanding (concepts such as electricity, forces, dissolving, how plants grow). The second part is scientific enquiry, which is about children working and thinking like a scientist.

The school science policy

A science policy is a short statement that reflects the national curriculum for that country and the views of the school about science education and how science is organised and taught throughout the school. It is a requirement for every school to have a policy statement. It forms part of the school's curriculum portfolio and is approved by governors and it is a public document.

A scheme of work for science

Phipps, R. (1997: 22) writes:

> A scheme of work is not a policy but an outline of a sequence of planned learning deemed essential for children's science education and can act as a management tool providing rapid access to teaching intentions and resources. From it the class teacher can derive more detailed lesson plans relevant to his/her needs.

Smith, C. (1998: 115) writes that a scheme of work:

> gives the school an agreed programme of work which outlines:

- the content
- the approach
- the teaching and learning, and
- the assessment of science, that will be followed by all teachers in the school.

Schools have schemes of work for science to ensure that there is a balanced programme across the school, which ensures that children's experiences of science are organised in such a way that they progress at an appropriate pace and level from year to year. Teachers use the science scheme of work rather like a 'big picture' which gives them an overview of where children are going from week to week; they then translate that overview into detailed lesson plans. Some schools develop their own scheme of work based on the needs of the children, expertise of the staff, and local resources such as parks, industry, woodland, seashore.

What does your school use? If you work in England, you might, for example, have seen the QCA scheme of work for science. The teachers you work with might use it in any one of the following ways:

- as the basis for all of their lessons, using the material without making changes;
- as a basis for their lessons, but where appropriate changing the activities to suit the children and resources in the school;
- for ideas of the kinds of activities they could use in a topic, picking and choosing activities they want to use.

Get to know the scheme of work for science that your school uses, particularly the parts of the scheme that are appropriate to the year groups with which you are working. This will help you to have an understanding of the wider picture in relation to what children are learning in science in that year group, and also what the children have already experienced in the previous year group.

Lesson plans

Science lesson plans outline the details of teaching and learning for a particular lesson. When teachers plan their individual science lessons they have to consider many things.

When planning a science lesson, teachers usually think about most of following questions:

- What do I want the children to learn?
- What do they already know?
- What do I need to teach them?
- What kind of practical activities could they do?
- Which aspect might they find difficult?
- What equipment and resources will we need?
- What scientific language will they need to use or learn?
- What questions do I need to ask?
- Can all the children do this, or do I need different activities for different children?
- Will they need to write about their science? What about those children who have difficulty writing?
- How will I organise the children?
- How will I know what they have learned at the end of the lesson?

Before working with children in science ask the teacher to share his or her science lesson plans with you so that you know the nature and format of the lesson. This will ensure that you have a clear understanding of the lesson and can discuss your role of supporting the teacher and children.

Using a lesson plan

Table 2.1 (pp. 14–17) is a sample lesson plan, annotated with explanations of the various parts of the plan and suggestions for the teaching assistant.

What does the lesson plan not always show?

If lesson plans told the whole story of a lesson it might be the length of a book! The reason a teacher writes a lesson plan is to think through what the lesson will

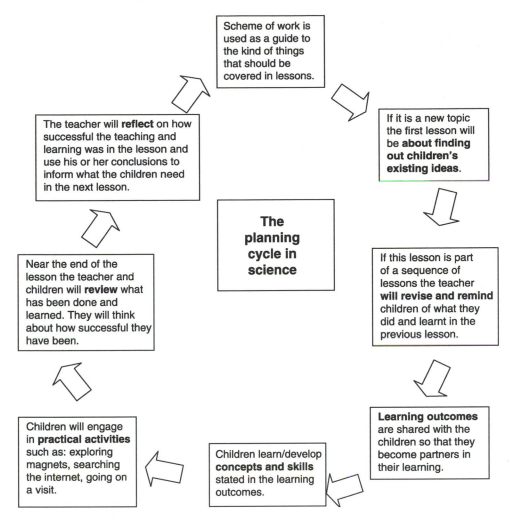

Figure 2.1 The planning cycle in science

be like, plan what the children will do, and to be aware of any issues that might arise. It attempts to tell the story of the flow of the lesson. A lesson plan helps the teacher to rehearse his or her lesson and, in doing so, helps the teacher to think and rethink the teaching and learning. A lesson plan should be detailed enough to ensure that during a teacher's absence someone else would know how to take the lesson.

There are, however, some things that teachers do not write down in detail. The teaching assistant needs to look out for these and talk them through with the teacher. These include:

● resources

● learning outcomes

● time frames.

Resources

The teacher might make a note of the resources required for most of the class but not necessarily specific resources that might need to be created or collected for supporting the group that you are working with. You should negotiate with your

Table 2.1 A sample lesson plan for science

Lesson plan		Comments
Subject: Science	**Year group: 1 Date: 17 January 2006**	
Ability group: Number of groups:	Levelled by ability 5 Red: High Ability Yellow: High Average Ability Green: Low Average Ability Orange: Low Ability Blue: SEN	
Number of children:	30	
Special educational needs/behaviour/ Gifted and talented notes	JS, LG – Poor behaviour on the carpet SB – profoundly deaf	The teaching assistant can support learning by: ● Taking LG to work somewhere else. Maybe this child does not need to be on the carpet. ● Praising LG when this child is on task. If you are supporting SB: ● Get everyone in the group to face SB and not all talk at once. Demonstrate the activity. ● Offer simple instructions to SB, if this child can read. ● Make sure that SB understands the task; do not underestimate the child or do the task for the child. Remember that science group work can be difficult for deaf children.
Learning objectives	Teacher Focus group on rotation (Green, Yellow, Red and Orange) Teaching assistant support group (Blue) Sc1 – scientific enquiry ● Collect evidence by making observations to answer questions. ● Ask questions and decide how they might find answers to them. ● Explore using the senses of sight and taste as appropriate, and make and record observations. ● Communicate what happened in a variety of ways.	The first set of learning objectives link to the National Curriculum strand in science where children develop ways of scientific thinking and working.

Lesson plan		Comments
	• To make simple comparisons and identify simple patterns or associations. • Review their work and explain what they did to others.	
	Sc2 – Humans and other animals • 2b – that humans and other animals need water to stay alive. • 2g – about the senses that enable humans to be aware of the world around them.	The second set of learning objectives link to National Curriculum strand where children develop scientific understanding about concepts related to what humans and other animals need to stay alive.
Activity	**Introduction** Read the story 'Thank you for a drink of water'. Discuss the book and how water is piped into our homes. Show the children the letters from the head teacher. Discuss with the children where they get water from in school. Discuss the new water machines installed in school recently. Then explain the independent task.	The teaching assistant can support learning by: • Making sure that you are familiar with the story. Ask the teacher if you can borrow the book prior to the lesson. If possible, ask the teacher to make sure that there are always two copies of books used, so that you can use it with your group when appropriate. Have copies of the letters from the head teacher to share with the children.
	Main activity Each group works with the teacher for about 10 minutes on a rotational basis. On the table is the equipment to use during the session. This includes fizzy bottled water, lemon flavoured water, strawberry flavoured water, peach water and cold filtered tap water. There are also drinking cups and recording slips. The children have a letter from the head teacher. Read the letter with the children. The letter is asking the children to decide which water the head teacher should get for the children. Ask the children to think how they can decide which water is the best, using the equipment in front of them. Hopefully the children will suggest tasting the water or smelling the water. Re-inforce the children are using their senses. Then test the water with the children. Use the recording sheets to write the children's responses.	The teaching assistant can support learning by: • Helping children read the letter. Encourage them to think about how they will answer the problem. They might need to be directed to look at the resources that have been put out and think how they might be used. • Help children record their results, or even re-create the record sheet if you think it is not appropriate for the children.

Lesson plan		Comments
Vocabulary	water life humans animals alive senses taste smell filtered	The teaching assistant can support learning by: ● modelling these words and then challenging children to use them when talking and writing.
Independent work	**Sc1 – Scientific enquiry** ● Use research material to collect information and record findings appropriately. **Sc3 – Materials and their properties** ● Find the many uses of water. The children work individually. They have to use the research materials on the table to find uses of water. Then using the materials on the table such as coloured pencils and cut out shapes they have to produce a poster to show the different uses of water. The children also have word cards to help with their recording. The task is differentiated by outcome.	The teaching assistant can support learning by: ● challenging children who are confident writers to be concise ● challenging all children to think about what are the most important things to put on the poster ● reminding children of the original letter.
Plenary	Ask the children to come together and ask them to describe what they did and what they found out. Ask the children how we can report back to the head teacher. Discuss the benefits of talking to her or writing to her. Before the children report back to the head teacher discuss the price tags on the water containers. Discuss with the children why the flavoured water and the fizzy water are more expensive. Discuss the implications of the head teacher having to buy more expensive drinks. Finally, write their reply to the head as a class shared writing activity. If short of time, this may be carried out in a future literacy lesson.	The teaching assistant can support learning by: ● practising what children might say when everyone is asked to describe what they did and what they found out (before the plenary). Children will be able to report back with more confidence. Writing up science activities is a legitimate use of literacy time, providing that the science writing is based on the content of the literacy lesson.
Support/ differentiation	Blue Group – support with reading and recording. Keep them focused on the investigation. Teaching assistant to work with this group. Red, Yellow, Green and Orange groups – teacher to observe the children's investigative skills, avoiding teacher-led practical investigation.	The teacher has identified the teaching assistant's role: to support reading and recording. Discussion with children will be an important aspect of your work. This helps children to clarify ideas, rehearse what they want to say and write.

Lesson plan		Comments
Resources	'Thank you for a drink of water' by Patricia and Victor Smeltzer. Flavoured bottled water, fizzy bottled water, water from the water cooler. Price tags. Cups for each child. Letter from the head teacher, containing the problem to solve. Recording sheets. Paper shapes, poster sheet and topic books. Reference books about water.	The teaching assistant can support learning by: • collecting resources before the lesson begins or having one or two children collect them • not choosing things for the children; this will help them develop independence.
Links to other subjects	PSHE Numeracy	
Health and safety issues	Ensure each child has his or her own cup.	To prevent the spread of germs, children must have their own cups.

teacher what kind of resources you might need to collect or prepare to support children's learning in science.

Don't be afraid to discuss with your teacher any ideas that you have in relation to preparing materials such as worksheets, games and other support material. Your teacher will be delighted that you are taking the initiative by customising support material tailored to the needs of individuals.

Lesson outcomes

Teachers are expected to share lesson outcomes (objectives) with the children, so that children know what they are going to learn and can, at the end of a lesson, with the teacher, reflect on whether they have been successful. There are different ways that teachers do this. Some give the children a list of learning objectives to put in their books at the beginning of a topic and as they are taught the children tick them off.

Time frames

Talk to the teacher about time managing the children so that activities are completed. While we do not want to place children under stress to finish, we do need to make sure that they do not dawdle. If some children take too long to complete their science it may be for several reasons. For example:

- Recording may be taking too long because it is inappropriate and needs changing. Discuss with the teacher what kind of recording methods might be more appropriate, particularly if the children have limited written skills. Could the children take photographs, draw pictures, use a table or sort items into sets?

- Children may go off task because they are unable to sustain an extended period of concentration. Could the task be broken down into shorter, manageable activities for these children? This would allow them some success and motivate them to move on to the next aspect.

The teaching assistant's role in the science lesson

To support the children's learning as much as possible it is essential that you understand what is going to happen in the lesson. You might want to ask the teacher for a suggested time frame for the lesson. It would be helpful for you to know:

- how long the introduction will last;

- how much time the children will have to complete the practical activities;

- when the clearing up should be done, with the children ready for the plenary;

- whether there will be any time during the week for children to complete unfinished work.

Ask the teacher for a prompt sheet relating to your role in the lesson. This could include learning outcomes or objectives, time frames, questions and key vocabulary and would help you be more effective in your role.

Do arrange time with your teacher to discuss anything that you do not understand about the lesson. While you might not like to interrupt the teacher and worry about taking up your teacher's time, it is essential that you clarify anything that you do not understand if you are to be effective in your role.

Science lessons should follow on from each other. They are part of a series of lessons that gradually develop children's scientific knowledge and understanding and their ability to work and think scientifically. Your role is to make sure that you make links on behalf of the teacher and for the children between the lessons. One of the most important things that you can do is to spend a few minutes talking with children about the previous lesson and what they remember, which new words they learnt, and explaining to them how the lesson builds on from the last lesson where appropriate.

To understand school planning and take part in lessons, ask yourself the following:

- Do you know the part of the school scheme of work for science that your teacher uses?

- Have you read the lesson plan so that you know the nature and format of the lesson and your role in supporting the teacher and children?

- Have you got a prompt sheet to support your role in the science lesson?

- Have you discussed anything that you do not understand or anything you want to suggest with your teacher?

- Have you organised the resources you will be using to support children's learning in science?

REMEMBER

- Schools use schemes of work and lesson plans to help them develop teaching and learning across the school in science.

- You might need to be proactive in asking your teacher to share lesson plans with you.

- You will need to discuss your role in the lesson with the teacher to make sure that you can provide the best support for the children in the science lesson.

CHAPTER 3

Effective questioning

In this chapter we will explore:

- why questioning is important in science;
- questioning in the science curriculum;
- different kinds of questions;
- using scientific language in questions;
- creating an effective questioning environment.

Why questioning is important in science

Asking questions is what science is all about. It is the central thing that scientists do. Think about some famous scientists. The questions they asked themselves led to amazing discoveries and had a huge impact on human beings.

Have you ever given or received blood? If you have, it is thanks to questions asked by Charles Drew (1904–1950). He was a black American scientist who asked this important question: Can we preserve blood so that it can be used later for someone else?

Drew's question led him to develop a system for the storing of blood plasma (a blood bank) that revolutionised the medical profession. He also established the American Red Cross blood bank and organised the supply of blood plasma to the British during the Second World War.

Isaac Newton (1643–1727) was an English scientist who asked questions about how the planets orbited around the Sun and about gravity and developed his theory of Universal Gravitation – 'gravity' to you and me. Perhaps his questions were:

- *Why doesn't the Moon fly away from the Earth?*
- *What makes the planets orbit in the same way?*
- *Why do things fall down to the ground when they are dropped?*

Alexander Fleming (1881–1955) was a scientist who asked a question that led to one of the most important medical discoveries in the world. One day in his laboratory he noticed that mould had developed accidentally on a staphylococcus culture plate. Staphylococcus bacteria cause many forms of infection, including food poisoning and wound infections. What was even more interesting was that the mould had created a bacteria-free circle around itself. What questions might Fleming have asked? He probably asked himself:

- *If I tried this again would the same thing happen?*
- *How can I make large amounts of this mould?*
- *How can we use it as a medicine?*
- *What should I call this?*

Fleming called the substance penicillin.

Professor Susan Greenfield is a modern-day scientist who asks questions about the brain and researches how the brain works. She focuses on such illnesses as Parkinson's disease and Alzheimer's disease. What sort of questions do you think she asks? Perhaps these are some of them:

- *What happens in the brain when someone develops Parkinson's or Alzheimer's disease?*
- *Does the brain change?*
- *If the brain changes what can be done to stop those changes and prevent these diseases in humans?*

DuPont scientist Joseph C. Shivers invented DuPont's spandex fibre in 1959 which has become the basis for Lycra. Today Lycra is used in clothing, from trousers to swimsuits and sportswear. This material can stretch and return to its original shape and be used with other materials such as cotton, wool, silk and nylon.

So what questions might Mr Shivers have asked? Were they:

- *What can this material do?*
- *What could it be used for?*
- *How far will it stretch?*
- *What shall we call it?*
- *Could the company make money from this?*

If scientists stopped asking questions then there would be no new developments in medicine, fabrics, engineering, food, space travel, farming, etc. So one of the most important aspects of science is the ability to ask a range of questions as well as find answers to them. If we want children to engage in science, and think and work like scientists, then we must support them in developing their ability to ask questions. The rest of this chapter is about how teaching assistants can develop approaches in this aspect of teaching and learning in science.

Questioning and the science curriculum

In following the science curriculum children:

- ask a range of questions;
- ask questions about science;
- use scientific vocabulary when asking questions;
- are able to ask questions that can be investigated;
- are able to understand that different questions may require different ways of finding answers.

The classroom, in fact the whole school environment, should be a place where children's questions are encouraged and valued. Teachers and others supporting children in their learning need to be effective questioners themselves. One of the first things we need to do is think carefully about the quality of our own questions. Different questions lead to different kinds of responses; some will make children think, others will take them into an activity. So we have to think carefully and ask the *right question* to make sure we achieve the learning outcomes we are working towards.

Different kinds of questions

The first word or two in a question is called a stem. Question stems include:

- who
- what
- where
- why

- would
- could
- what if
- how

- when
- should
- which
- did.

There are many question stems. We need to make sure that we use many of them to expose children to their variety. Different question stems lead to different kinds of questions, which in turn prompt children do different things in science.

Questions that focus attention

This type of question can help to focus children's attention on detail, for example, in a picture, object or something that happens. Often teachers begin by asking about gross features. For example when looking at a real spider or a picture of one, the teacher might ask:

- *What shape is the spider?*
- *How many parts does the body have?*
- *How many legs does the spider have?*

Then the teacher might move on to questions about details, for example:

- *Are the legs jointed?*
- *What can you see on the spider's legs?*
- *What are the eyes like?*
- *What do you think is at the front of the head?*

Questions that focus attention can also be used when children are using the other senses, for example:

- What does the tree bark feel like, rough or smooth?
- Is the whole bark rough?
- What does the piece under your finger feel like?
- What kind of sound is that, loud or quiet?
- How does the sound change?
- What do you think is making the sound?

Open and closed questions

Closed questions lead to a yes/no or purely factual answer. For example:

- Do you like cheese? Yes
- How tall are you? 154 centimetres
- Is this a plant or an animal? Plant
- Does a wooden ruler conduct electricity? No

There is no right or wrong answer to an open question however, and such questions are used to encourage children to explain their own ideas. For example:

- What do you think the weather will be like next week?
- Why do you prefer this smell to that smell?

SOMETHING TO THINK ABOUT

Test yourself – Which questions are open? Which are closed?

1. How long do you think the ice will take to melt?
2. What kind of animal eats meat?
3. Which is the best fabric for teddy's raincoat?
4. What colour is a ladybird?
5. What are the names of the colours in a rainbow?
6. How do you think you could find out which elastic stretches the furthest?

Answers 1. Open; 2. Closed; 3. Open; 4. Closed; 5. Closed; 6. Open

Measurement questions

Measurement questions put a number to an observation. If you tell someone who has never met you that you are tall, what would that person imagine? Someone who was 172 cm (5 ft 6 ins)? Someone who was 198 cm (6 ft 6 ins)? The word 'tall' doesn't give an accurate measurement. But if you say that you are 175 cm (or 5 ft 8 ins) then they have a better idea of your height.

Measurement in science provides numbers that help us to understand quantities such as how much, how long, how many. Taking and recording measurements can help us to see patterns and relationships in data. For example, if we compare a list of children's heights in the classroom to children's shoe sizes, we could suggest that taller children have larger feet.

When using measurement questions it is important to use the right vocabulary, for example:

- How many *centimetres* tall are you?
- What is the *volume* of the water in the container?
- What do you think we should use to measure the *distance* that the car has travelled?

Comparison questions

Comparison questions are used to sort things into groups (classify), for example:

- Which materials are attracted to the magnet?
- Which materials are the stretchiest?
- Which materials dissolve in water?
- Which animals belong to the group that eat plants (are herbivores)?

Action questions

Action questions are used to encourage children to try things out. For example, if children are finding out about things that can stretch, you might ask:

- When you stretch the materials do they go back when you let them go?
- Which material stretches the furthest?

To find the answers to these questions the children will have to do something (in this case, stretch something). They might:

- collect a variety of stretchy and non-stretchy materials;
- find out what happens when they pull on elastic bands;
- test a variety of stretchy materials to find out which is the stretchiest.

> ## SOMETHING TO THINK ABOUT
>
> Preparing different kinds of questions – First, collect some magnets. You might find these on a fridge or handbag clasp or in a magnetic toy, knife-rack or can-opener. Next, think about different kinds of questions: open, closed, ones that focus attention, measurement, action and comparison. Now think of some questions in relation to your collection and jot these down. Share your questions with someone else, for example one of the teachers you work with or another teaching assistant. Hopefully you will have created a useful range of questions, and recognised how powerful it is to reflect on your own questioning ability.

Listening to the teacher asking questions

To develop as an effective questioner, it will help if you listen to how the teacher uses questions. The teacher's use of questions can provide a model for you.

When observing the teacher, think about the different kinds of questions he or she uses. How are children prompted to do different things? What is the sequence of questions? How are the children encouraged to develop their answers? You will learn to be an effective teacher by asking yourself:

- What kind of questions does the teacher ask?

- When does the teacher ask the questions?

- How does the teacher encourage children to respond?

- How does the teacher's body language change?

- How does the teacher praise children? Does this encourage them to answer? Are the children's questions valued?

- What does the teacher do if the children's answer is not quite what the teacher expected?

Using scientific language in questions

When you are modelling good questioning with children it is important to use correct scientific vocabulary. For example, if children know the word transparent and can use it, then you should use 'transparent' rather than an everyday word such as 'see-through'. Questions that use everyday vocabulary provide a lower level of challenge to children than those that use scientific vocabulary. Figure 3.1 contains examples of lower-level questions, with their more effective counterparts.

Lower-level question	Effective question
Which material can you see through?	Which material is transparent?
How do you know something is see-through?	What are the properties of a transparent material?
Why can't you see through bathroom windows?	Why are bathroom windows translucent or opaque?
How can you make plastic that is see-through/not see-through?	How can you make transparent plastic material translucent or opaque?

Figure 3.1 Questions that use everyday vocabulary and those that use scientific vocabulary

Creating an effective questioning environment

There are many ways that you can help to create an effective questioning environment in the science classroom. Here are some examples; some of which you might like to suggest to your class teacher that you create, if he or she has not come across them before.

Question prompt sheets

These are for your own purpose. They are a list of effective questions that you or your teacher has decided to ask. They are meant as a prompt only, to give you an idea of the kind of questions to ask. (Remember to use different question stems and use appropriate scientific language.) For example, if you are asking questions about circuits, your prompt sheet might look like this:

- How will you make your own switch for your circuit?
- What ideas have you got?
- How can you use what is on the table to help you?
- Remember how Mrs Smith showed you how to make a switch, what did she use?
- Do you think it matters where you put the switch? Why?

Question postbox

Make a postbox that children can post their science questions into. (This could be the Christmas postbox or you could make a special one.) Encourage children to think about questions related to their science topic or anything scientific and to put these on paper or card you provide. Open the box and share and discuss the questions with the whole class once a week. (Remember, all questions are good ones!) Children might be able to answer some questions right away, or decide to look for the answers.

Question books

These are a big book of questions that children ask about their science topic (or the teacher or teaching assistant creates for the children). The children could be led through an activity with a sequence of questions. (Remember to leave space for children's work, photographs of children working, and so on.)

Interactive displays

These encourage children to use the display itself to look for answers, try activities such as sorting objects, label items, solve problems, add to it with items from home or talk and work with a friend about the science topic. Question mobiles are great for providing questions that will challenge children. You can hang mobiles from a ceiling or place them on a wall.

Whatever kind of display you use, you need to think about:

- What are the learning outcomes?
- What different question stems can I use?
- What do I want the children to do? (measure, problem-solve, compare?)
- What scientific language can I include?
- How can the children add their own questions?

SOMETHING TO THINK ABOUT

Preparing an effective questioning environment – Discuss your ideas about creating an effective questioning environment with the teacher. Agree with him or her that before your next class you will:

- create a question prompt sheet to help you ask the right question at the right time;
- create and use a question postbox (or interactive display, or question book or question mobile).

To encourage children to think, talk about and carry out practical activity, you need to give them thinking time to answer a question. Resist the temptation to jump in and answer for them or ask another child. When children are asked a question they have to:

- listen to the question;
- think about it and decide if they understand it;
- find links to what they already know or have experienced;
- work out an answer;
- then answer the question.

All of that takes time and we need to understand and respect this. We also need to recognise that sometimes children can help each other with questions. You could suggest that they work with their 'talk partner' to work out their answers.

Here's a list of questions you can ask yourself about your own use of questions. This list can help you check if you are questioning in the most effective way possible:

- Do you use different question stems and ask different kinds of questions?

- Have you listened to and thought about how the teacher uses questions?

- Do you model scientific language rather than everyday language?

- Do you create question prompt sheets for yourself?

- Have you created a question box, book, or mobile?

- Do you give children time to think through their answers when you are asking them questions?

REMEMBER

- Effective questioning is central to science.

- You need to reflect on how well you role model effective questions in science.

- Observing the class teacher and how he or she uses questions can help you to support children in science.

- You need to make sure that you focus on the learning outcomes and moving children forward in science when you ask questions.

CHAPTER 4

Supporting practical work

In this chapter we will explore:

- supporting learning before the lesson;
- supporting learning during the lesson;
- supporting learning after the lesson;
- managing behaviour.

The role of the teaching assistant in supporting practical work is simple: help them; do not do it for them (unless there is a safety issue). This is true whether the practical work is pouring liquid into a container, using a computer, measuring height or making an electric circuit. Practical activity is designed to help children develop scientific understanding, a range of skills and an ability to work with others and to share ideas. The two words that teachers and teaching assistants need to keep in mind are 'hands off' (unless the child really cannot manage without assistance).

Supporting learning before the lesson

It is important that you are fully prepared before the lesson starts. This can be difficult, particularly if you have been supporting children in another class, you are part-time or your class teacher is unable to talk to you before the lesson. Whatever the circumstances, you will be more effective in your role if you have been able to spend some time preparing for the lesson or activity.

Preparation is so crucial in science lessons because it can help you:

- have a greater understanding of the purpose of the lesson;
- check which aspects of subject knowledge you are least confident about;
- try out equipment or parts of an activity that you are unsure of, so that you are confident when working with the children;
- offer some of your own ideas, tailored to the children;
- check the timescale for working with your group;
- understand potential health and safety issues;
- bring up concerns you have with the teacher.

Your role might also include preparing materials for the lesson (ones your teacher has asked you to produce or you've offered based on your own ideas). There are a range of materials suggested in Chapter 8 that teaching assistants could provide to support science lessons. These include:

- word banks
- labels
- games
- worksheets adapted for the children
- additional equipment
- alternative activities and experiences.

A self-audit

To check if you've prepared for the lesson, ask yourself:

- Have I read the teacher's lesson plan?
- Do I know what the learning outcomes are for the whole class/for the child or children I am supporting?
- Has the teacher told me what to do during the lesson?
- Am I confident with my own scientific understanding?
- Have I tried out the activity so I know some of the challenges the children will face?
- Is the equipment for my group available and working?
- Do I know what the vocabulary for the lesson is?
- Is the support material ready?
- Do any of the children need special resources?

Supporting learning during the lesson

One of the most important things that teaching assistants should do during a science lesson is to observe and listen to the teacher. Watch what the teacher does, particularly if he or she demonstrates a way of working to the children, since you might have to repeat it with your group. Take note of the type of language the teacher uses, particularly scientific vocabulary, the questions asked and how the children are encouraged to respond and, in particular, how the teacher encourages children to share their ideas.

Maintaining and encouraging children's independence

If we think back to the first chapter of this book we'll remember that one of the key aspects of science teaching and learning was developing children's ability to be independent in the way they think and learn. This can be very difficult to do and the hardest part of it is resisting the temptation to take over and do the thinking and practical work for the children. This is the worst thing we can do and it is not the kind of support that the teacher or the children want or need.

Adapting activities to suit the children

You may need to adapt activities to suit the children that you are working with. This could include:

- Changing the activity. For example, if the rest of the class are carrying out investigations into 'dissolving sugars' but your group still does not know what 'dissolving' is, you could have them find out which things 'do and do not dissolve', such as marbles, sugar, coffee and sand.

- Offering additional experience to help understanding of a challenging concept. For example, you could help children experience friction by having them feel rough surfaces (which have a lot of friction) and smooth surfaces (which do not have much friction).

- Using different equipment. For example, if you are working with children who have visual impairments, you could use a buzzer in an electrical circuit instead of a light bulb so they know when their circuit is working.

- Using alternative worksheets. For example, if you are working with children who have reading difficulties, you could use worksheets with pictures or photographs rather than words.

- Using different ways of recording their science; for example, diagrams or strip cartoons.

Hands off!

Children love to be active and they enjoy science because of the hands-on practical activity that they engage with. Nothing could be worse for the child than having someone do it for them while they stand back and watch. No matter how slow some children are, let the children carry out the activity themselves.

For example, if children are classifying animals, allow them to put the animal where they think it should be and ask them to explain why they have put it in that set. You might find that their reason is very logical and acceptable according to their thinking or understanding. Also, let children take their own measurements. Stop them if they are not using equipment correctly, show them how to use it and let them continue. Do not try to rush children by doing things yourself if you are running out of time. The children will not learn anything. Instead, make a mental note to think about other ways of working next time you are with that group, ways that will enable them to complete the task in the given time.

Respect children's ideas

Children have their own ideas in science. These might not always be the best ideas or the most scientific ones, but they belong to the children and we should respect them. This means that sometimes we have to allow children to follow their own instincts even if we know they won't succeed. Children must be allowed to fail in science; they can learn a great deal from mistakes. (But children should not be placed in a position where they are always going to fail.) Sometimes children need to get it wrong so that their ideas are challenged and they have to think again. This is one of the ways that children's ideas change and move towards something that is more scientifically acceptable.

Listen to the children

Children have lots of ideas and they like to share them. Make sure children take it in turns to talk about or show what they are doing and insist that they listen and watch each other. Ask them to think about what others have said or done by using questions such as:

- What do you think of Yasmin's idea?
- What should Peter do after that?
- Who has a different idea?
- What other things do you think we could try?
- Which idea do you think will work best? Why?
- Would you please show everyone what you were doing? What do you all think about what John has just shown you?

When asking questions think back to Chapter 3 and what makes a good question. Asking fewer, more effective questions is much better than asking a lot of questions that have little impact.

Be a good role model

Think about what you do and say. For example:

- Use scientific language where appropriate and move children from using everyday to scientific language where necessary.
- Share learning outcomes. Tell children what you and they are going to do and why.
- Manage time. Keep telling children how much time they have to do a task. Use the class clock or another one, but make sure that the task is achievable in the time given.
- When demonstrating something, talk out loud as if explaining it to yourself. For example, 'Now I am going to pour the water into the container and measure the right volume, to keep the test fair. Next I am going to pour twenty grams of granulated sugar into the water . . .' This will explain the activity as well as share scientific language with the children.

Be prepared and have an additional activity

Children might finish early, in which case you will need to give them an activity such as a revision or extension activity. Word games or 'guess the object' are examples of activities that can reinforce learning. For example, if children complete a task on magnets early, you might ask them to:

- explore magnets that they haven't used;
- play a magnetic game like a magnets fishing game;
- look at and talk about some magnets you have brought from home, such as fridge magnets.

Make sure that the additional activity is fun and you praise children for completing their work early. They will then start to realise that there is a reward for completing tasks and become more motivated to finish activities.

Assess children's progress

Towards the end of the session you need to review what children have achieved by asking them to:

- think about the learning outcomes they were told about at the beginning of the lesson;
- discuss with their talk partner what they have learned;
- discuss with their talk partner the parts they found hard;
- think about what they liked and why;
- think about how confident they are about what they have learned; for example, if you ask children whether sound can travel through different materials they might signal that they know the answer by using a 'thumbs-up' ('thumbs-down' could tell you they don't understand and waving hands could tell you they are unsure).

A self-audit

To check if you've supported learning during the lesson, ask yourself:

- Do I keep my hands off, letting the children carry out activities?
- Do I respect the children's ideas?
- Do I listen to what the children are saying to me and to each other?
- Am I a good role model in how I talk and work?
- Am I prepared and do I have spare activities in case children complete their work early?
- Do I assess children's progress during the activity?

Supporting learning after the lesson

Hopefully your work with the children will have been a great success and you will have shared your delight with the children at how well they worked. You might have given individual children stars, stickers or merits to celebrate their success whether it be because they had good ideas, measured correctly, recorded using a table or took turns.

During the lesson you will have learned a lot about the children, for example:

- how they worked together;
- whether they used the equipment correctly;
- the kind of ideas they shared;
- how much they understood;
- how much of the activity they managed to complete;
- whether any children worked beyond or below their potential.

Any feedback you can offer to the teacher about the children working in science will be very useful. If you don't have time to feed back orally, jot a few notes down and leave them for your teacher to read.

Make sure that children have returned equipment to the correct place and stored any work they have done appropriately or given it to the teacher. Your teacher will find it a great help if you offer to place their work in a big book or use it as part of a classroom display.

Don't be afraid to suggest to your teacher what the children could do in the next lesson. After all, you have been working closely with them; the teacher will have been engaged elsewhere in the classroom with other children.

A self-audit

To check if you've supported learning after the lesson, ask yourself:

- Do I praise children and tell them how well they have worked?
- Do I provide oral or written feedback to the teacher?
- Have I, where appropriate, put children's work in a big book or on display?
- Do I make suggestions about where the children are in their learning and the direction in which they might need to go next?
- Do I take and display photographs of the children working?

Managing behaviour

Managing behaviour in science is no different than in any other area of the curriculum. One of the fallacies about science and, in particular, practical work, is that children will misbehave when they engage in hands-on, practical activities. The reality is that if the practical activities are well structured and within the capability of the children, they are less likely to display inappropriate behaviour. They will be actively involved and interested in their learning.

Why do children go off task?

There is always a reason why children are unwilling to engage in a task in science. Usually there is a very simple reason, and it is most frequently because the child is unsure about what to do. That might be because the child:

- does not have a sound understanding of the science concepts involved;
- does not manage to follow all of the teacher's instructions;
- does not understand what the teacher wants the class to do;
- lacks confidence to carry out practical activities;
- has English as an additional language.

Strategies for managing behaviour

Your school has probably put in place rules for behaviour already. It is your responsibility to know what these rules are. You must be prepared to enforce them and enforce specific classroom rules your teacher has made.

It will also be very helpful for you to be aware of things that might be affecting your children's behaviour:

- a child may have difficulty managing unfamiliar ideas or activities;
- a child may have learning difficulties or physical challenges;
- the interpersonal relations between children may not be good.

You might want to have your own set of rules as well, for work with you or at your table. If so, it is a good idea to develop this with the children. Base it on positive responses, for example:

We are brilliant scientists because we:

- *Listen to each other*
- *Share our ideas*
- *Think about what each other says*
- *Use equipment carefully*
- *Take turns*
- *Stick to our own jobs*
- *Put things away carefully*
- *Work safely*

Where children work in a group you could give each child a badge that says what their role is, such as 'Chief measurer', 'Chief recorder', 'Chief observer', 'Chief doer', and so on.

Here are some strategies for effective behaviour management:

- Observe and analyse – look at children who are not working constructively and how the teacher responds to those children. Think about why the children are behaving the way they are, then decide upon the most appropriate action.

- Intervene early – watch for tell-tale signs of imminent misbehaviour (this could be a child reaching for some equipment that he or she does not need), and distract them as soon as possible.

- Sit close to a child who misbehaves, smiling and engaging the child in activity.

- Remove equipment if it is not needed so that children are not distracted by it.

- Give the child a positive role – you could say, 'Today you are in charge of measuring. That is a very important job and I know that you can be sensible and do it very carefully'.

- Praise, praise, praise, and reward positive behaviour – for example, with stickers or stars.

- Let the children know what you want – be clear in your instructions, breaking them into small steps if necessary.

- Check children's understanding and make sure that the activity is not too difficult.

- Ask the children to show you what to do.

Keeping children on task

There are several strategies you can use if you think children are likely to go off task:

- Explanation and demonstration – Explain the activity again and ask the child to do it with you. Demonstrate the activity to the children and talk about what you are doing as you do it and ask the children to tell you what you are doing.

- Modelling – You can do this with photos or cards. Do the activity yourself before the lesson and take digital photographs of the main steps (or write these on separate cards). Before the activity, ask the children to put the photos in the right order. You could also ask them to explain what is happening in each step.

- Break the task down into steps – Smaller steps can be more easily managed and give children opportunities to achieve quite quickly. The sense of accomplishment as they complete each step boosts their self-esteem and confidence and helps with the next.

- Trial and error – Let the children try out their ideas (using the resources) before they actually carry out the activity. They could do a trial before a fair test, for example. This allows them to rehearse ideas, make mistakes and work out how to do something correctly before they do the real thing.

- Observation and challenge – If you have a more-able group (or if your group is working very well), it might be more effective just to observe them, challenging them to explain what they are doing, how they solved their problem.

REMEMBER

- Listen to the children.
- Observe the children and learn what they can do and what they know.
- Keep you hands off! Allow children to develop independence.
- Praise even the smallest achievement; it might be a giant step for the child.

Developing children's ideas in science

In this chapter we will explore:

- what are scientific concepts;
- how teachers find out what children know;
- how to support the development of children's ideas in science.

What are scientific concepts?

Scientific concepts are ideas about science. Some concepts, such as forces, are complex; others, such as magnets, are easier for children to understand. Of course the concepts children develop about science are less complex than those developed by someone studying physics at university, but children still require support in developing their ideas.

The development of children's concepts relies on their making sense of lots of different experiences – from school, home, friends, television and everyday life. There are many things that can influence how children develop their understanding of the world. Because of this, some of the ideas that they have might not be scientifically sound.

Does this matter? Not really – why should young children who have had a limited experience of making sense of the world be expected to understand how science works? Children start to make sense of the world at their own pace and will gradually begin to think more scientifically.

The role of the teacher and teaching assistant in supporting this change is crucial. You can help by understanding children's existing ideas in science and by using a range of approaches to help children think more scientifically.

How teachers find out what children know

In science there are a number of established ways that teachers find out what children know, in order to decide on more appropriate ways of supporting children in their learning.

Drawings

To find out how differently children think, you can ask them to draw something that is unknown to them. For instance, you can give them an outline of a figure and ask them to draw the figure's skeleton. You can then compare the children's drawings with an accurate drawing.

This simple activity can help us appreciate the fact that we might think we know what children think and how they view the world but we are not always right. It makes us realise that it is important to elicit what children think so that we can find appropriate ways to support them. One child's drawing may be different (perhaps quite different) from another child's. In this case, if the children's ideas were very different to what we know about the skeleton we would try changing their ideas of the skeleton by challenging those ideas, for example:

- getting children to feel where their bones are;
- bringing in a model skeleton for children to explore;
- showing video clips of human and animal skeletons;
- reading books like *Funny Bones* by Allan and Janet Ahlberg

Concept maps

A concept map is used to encourage children to show what they know by making links between different words or pictures.

In the concept map shown in Figure 5.1, the children were given words related to the topic of plastic. The teacher gave the children a set of words and they glued the words onto a sheet of paper. Next they looked at the words and used their

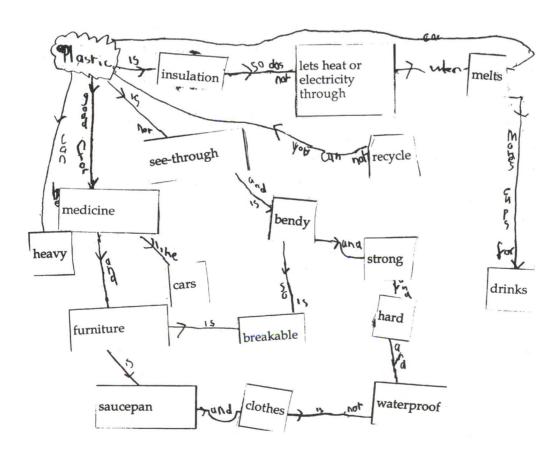

Figure 5.1 Concept map about plastic

knowledge of plastic as a material to draw lines between them and then wrote comments on the lines to help explain the links that they had made.

> ## SOMETHING TO THINK ABOUT
>
> Look at the concept map in Figure 5.1. What does the child who drew this map know about plastic? Make a list of your ideas and a second list of the areas where you think the child's ideas are limited or wrong (these are often called misconceptions or alternative ideas).

The child who drew the concept map shown in Figure 5.1 has some good ideas about plastic, such as: 'Plastic *is* insulation *so does not* lets heat or electricity through'. From this we know that the child understands that plastic is a thermal insulator (it does not let heat through) and an electrical insulator (does not let electricity through).

However, the child also makes a link that suggests knowledge and understanding is not secure: 'Plastic *you can not* recycle'. The child needs to be challenged on this idea and helped to understand the concept that some plastics *can be* recycled.

Concept cartoons

Concept cartoons were developed by Brenda Keogh and Stuart Naylor and are used in many schools to elicit children's ideas in science and find out what their scientific understanding is about everyday situations. In concept cartoons, characters express their understanding of a concept; their ideas may be right or wrong. Children are asked if they agree or disagree with characters and explain why. Figure 5.2 is an example of a concept cartoon that is used with both children and adults.

Figure 5.2   Concept cartoon of a snowman (Keogh and Naylor 1996, p. 66)

Many children agree with the statement *'Don't put the coat on the snowman – it will melt him'* – probably because we tell children to put on a coat 'to keep warm' when they go out to play on a cold day. So some children will think that putting a coat on the snowman will make it melt. What actually happens is that the coat insulates the snow – it keeps the cold inside the coat. Heat from outside does not transfer (move through the material) to melt the snow.

Of course, it is no good knowing about children's alternative ideas (as they are sometimes called), if we don't do anything about them. So what can we do? One thing we can do is help them test their ideas. To find out if wrapping something cold in fabric makes it warmer or colder, children could wrap some ice cubes in fabric and leave some ice cubes unwrapped – and see which ice cubes melt faster.

Having the children run a test lets them find out for themselves if their ideas are right. Simply telling them the correct answer is not an appropriate way forward – children need to experience what happens for themselves. When the children see that the wrapped ice cubes do not melt as quickly as the unwrapped cubes, their original idea is challenged and they are more likely to develop more scientifically sound ideas. It is worth noting that some children will not accept their ideas being challenged and will hold on firmly to their original idea, sometimes until they are much older (even into adulthood).

Thought showers

Another way for teachers to find out what children know is simply to ask them something and have them tell you what they know. What they say gets written down as a 'thought shower' of statements or ideas. Figure 5.3 is one class's thought shower about healthy eating.

Once they have a list of ideas from children, teachers have to decide which ideas need challenging and what experiences or activities will help move children's understanding towards the more scientifically acceptable. In the example of the thought shower, you could have children research the topic and find information from different sources such as books, videos, leaflets, CD-Roms

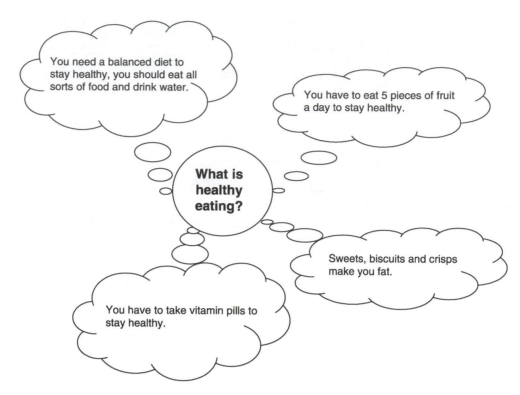

Figure 5.3　A thought shower about healthy eating

or the internet, invite a dietician or health visitor to talk to the children or have the children write to Jamie Oliver for advice about healthy eating.

Collections

Collections are a good way of finding out how children understand sets or groups of things. For example, if you want to find out if children know about the characteristics of insects, you could give them a collection of invertebrates (mini-beasts) and ask them to make sets of insects. If they put invertebrates with six legs, two pairs of wings and three parts to their body in one set, you could conclude that their concept of insects is good. However, if they put a spider, millipede and woodlouse together in one set it would be clear that their understanding of the characteristics of insects is not very advanced.

Listening to children

Asking children questions and listening to them talk is one of the most important ways of finding out what they know. However, we must be careful not to underestimate the sense that children can make of their world. Here is a lovely example from a friend:

> I was walking along with my grandson who is nearly three years old. We were talking about the plane that was high in the sky and wondering where it was going, when Thomas said, 'You know, Grandpa, that plane isn't really small. I know because it was bigger than me when I was in it going to Spain.'

How wonderfully perceptive was the child's comment and how advanced his thinking!

Children continually make their own sense of the world around them and their ideas deserve respect – sometimes admiration. Here's an example of a child explaining something to the teacher without understanding the science of it:

Teacher: *Do you know what happens to the Sun at night?*
Child: *It goes behind the hills until morning.*

We know that the child's explanation is not scientifically sound, but it is an accurate reflection of the child's experience. At this time in her life, this is the best sense the child can make of what is happening. Her personal experience is of watching the sky or cartoons on the television. As she grows up and has more experience and learns more about the planets, her ideas will change and move closer to what we know is correct.

How to support the development of children's ideas in science

Supporting the development of children's ideas in science is crucial. Here are some suggestions of how you can be effective in your role:

- listen carefully to children;

- respect children's ideas;

- develop children's confidence to tell you what they think;

- try to understand how children have constructed their ideas;

- ask children to explain what makes them think that, or ask what have they seen that has helped to form their idea;

- ask them effective questions to clarify their thinking and your understanding of their views, for example 'How do you know that?', 'What have you seen that makes you think that?';

- observe how your teacher elicits children's ideas and how your teacher responds to them;

- find alternative ways of explaining things to children;

- give children 'hands-on' experience which will help to challenge and develop their ideas;

- get to know common misconceptions, watch out for them in children, and with your teacher find ways of dealing with them

You should share your experiences with the class teacher, to help you and the teacher understand how and what children are thinking. This provides an important and powerful platform for deciding the next step in the teaching and learning process. It will help the teacher to decide what kind of experiences will help to develop the concept further. It also provides an opportunity for you to discuss with the teacher the nature of children's ideas that are not scientifically correct. This may even help to clarify your own thinking.

REMEMBER

- Children sometimes have different ideas to those that are scientifically accepted.

- We should respect children's ideas in science and realise that they come from the child's personal experience, which is different to ours.

- Observe how the teacher elicits children's ideas and how the teacher challenges them, and be patient – children's ideas do not always change because of one activity.

CHAPTER 6

Using scientific language

In this chapter we will explore:

- language in science;
- spelling strategies from literacy;
- children's experience of scientific vocabulary;
- children's writing about science.

Language in science

Learning to speak and write is a continuous process of progression for children and the primary school years are particularly important. Some children are more competent and confident than others in science. All children will be in the position of being challenged to use different ways of recording and learn strange scientific words. Science can make life difficult for children because some of the new words they have to learn (such as 'force') have everyday meanings. No wonder some children find writing in science challenging and need additional support. This chapter looks at some of the main issues related to supporting language in science; the next chapter examines how children use writing to communicate about science in different ways.

Science has very a specific language. For some people it is a bit like a foreign language that they have to learn. Scientific language is acquired as children:

- listen to the words used;
- use the five senses to find out what the word means (where appropriate);
- experience the word in different contexts;
- practise using the word;
- see the word in written form.

There are five 'golden rules' for learning scientific language:

1 Say the word.
2 Read the word.
3 Know what the word means.
4 Give examples of the word in everyday life.
5 Write the word down.

For example, if you are teaching the word 'flexible', children should:

1 Say the word 'flexible'.

2 Read the word 'flexible'.

3 Know that the word 'flexible' means something that can be easily bent.

4 Use the word 'flexible' to describe things such as pipe-cleaners, plastic rulers.

5 Write the word 'flexible' and learn how to spell it.

To make sure that they really understand the word you could ask the children to give you an example of something that is not flexible, for example, a rock.

Spelling strategies from literacy

Literacy is about using and developing children's ability to talk, read and write in all aspects of life. Strategies used to support learning literacy (and other areas of the curriculum) can be easily transferred to science. Spelling strategies are important because children need to learn how to read and spell scientific words.

Here are some strategies that you might use in literacy to support children's learning of a scientific vocabulary.

- Scientific dictionaries and glossaries – Children could make their own scientific dictionary which they refer to when experiencing difficulty with a word. You might create, with the whole group, a glossary or dictionary of technical words for one science topic.

- LSCWC – Look, Say, Cover, Write, Check.

- Buddy systems – Give pairs of children flash cards with scientific words on them and ask them to test each other on the spellings. You could also ask them to test each other on the meanings, having given them them flash cards with a definition of the word on the back.

- Word banks and flash cards – Cards or sheets with the key words for that topic. See Figure 6.1 for two examples.

Word bank	Word bank
Electricity	**Plant reproduction**
battery	sepal
bell	petal
bulb	stigma
bulb holder	stamen
buzzer	anther
cell	ovary
circuit	filament
clip	style
component	carpel
conductor	
crocodile	A *stamen* is an *anther* and a *filament*
diagram	
insulator	A *carpel* is a *stigma* and a *style* and an *ovary*
motor resistance	
resistor switch	
wire	

Figure 6.1 Word banks or flash cards on electricity and plant production

Children's experience of scientific vocabulary

Physically experiencing scientific words is very important for all children, but in particular for those children with language difficulties, children who have English as a second language and those children who have hearing or visual impairments. When children are learning new scientific words, try to provide opportunity for them to actually experience the word. For example:

- Pull – Ask the children to gently pull each other. Sit a child in a large box with a rope handle and ask children to try to pull the box.

- Friction – Give children some glass-paper (sandpaper) and very smooth paper or fabric. Ask the children to compare and describe the texture of the two materials. Ask them to rub different materials together (i.e., rough and rough, rough and smooth, smooth and smooth) and describe the different sensations.

- Transparent – Give children lots of objects that are transparent and opaque and ask them to describe what they can and cannot see when they look through the objects.

- Melt – Give children a chocolate button to hold in their hand. Eventually it will melt in their hands; this will help them understand what the word melt means.

- Upthrust – Get children to put a balloon in a tank or bowl of water. Ask them to push the balloon down into the water and describe what they can feel. Talk with them about how they can feel the water pushing the balloon back up, making it difficult for them to keep the balloon down in the water.

- Vibration – Ask children to put their fingers against their own throat and hum. They will feel the vibration from their voice-box. Tap a tuning fork and hold it against the cheek of a child. The child will feel the fork making their cheek tingle.

Having fun with scientific words

We need to try many different ways to support children in learning these new scientific words. Here are some fun ways for children to get to know new words. Ask the children to:

- say the word quietly, shout it and sing it;

- say the word so that it sounds like what it means, for example, 'elastic' could be 'eee . . . lllllllll . . . aaaaaaaaaa . . . sssssssss . . . tic';

- say the word and make hand signs to explain the word, for example, pretend to stretch a jumper for 'stretch' or pull an elastic band and let it snap back for 'pull'.

Mixing words up

Children and adults sometimes get confused and mix scientific ideas and words up. A common mistake is to mix up 'melting' with 'dissolving':

- *Melting* is when a substance is heated and the molecules begin to move (vibrate) to such an extent that they break away and the substance begins to flow. Different substances can melt at different temperatures, such as chocolate and ice (frozen water). Ice, chocolate, cheese, wax and butter are all examples of things that melt, and children will be familiar with these and you can show them melting in the classroom.

- *Dissolving* is when a substance is placed in liquid, for example, salt into water. The water breaks down the salt into smaller components and these fit within the molecules of the water, making it look as though the salt has disappeared; it is still there though in the water.

Scientific and everyday words

There are lots of words in science that have an 'everyday' as well as scientific meaning and lots of everyday words that can sound scientific, which can be very confusing to young children. (A couple of howlers are the child thinking 'gravity' is 'what you put on your dinner' and 'friction' is 'a book you read'!).

When you are introducing new scientific vocabulary:

- don't assume the children know what the word means;

- always ask children what *they* think the word means *before* you tell them what it means.

Be prepared for children who are gifted and talented to correct you by giving you the more precise word for something (for example, 'cell' for '1.5V battery' or 'scapula' for 'shoulder blade'!). You might want to learn some new words yourself, so as to challenge children who are more able and who enjoy new words.

Do not be afraid to challenge children by having them use scientific words. It is part of your job to do this so that they will:

- become familiar with the words;

- spell scientific words;

- use scientific words in the correct context;

- enjoy using scientific words;

- become confident and competent in using scientific words.

Children's writing about science

With regard to supporting children's writing, Edwards, S. (2004: 28) says that teaching assistants:

> can support at all levels. We need to start children off with healthy attitudes and perceptions of writing. In my view there are three main strands:
>
> - To guide – sensitively and with regard to the pace of individual learning.
> - To model – allow learners to see good examples of what is required.
> - To facilitate – through a positive learning environment.

Each of the points that Edwards makes can be applied to supporting children's writing in science. Children should talk first and then write. They need to:

- think about what they know or have done;
- talk, so that they can articulate and hear their own thoughts;
- then write things down.

It is therefore important that children are given lots of opportunities to talk in science:

- to you, the teaching assistant;
- to the teacher;
- to others in the group;
- to their talk partners.

First, children should be given opportunities to think through what they have done and their ideas. Then they should be supported in writing down in concise sentences what they have talked about. The most useful piece of equipment for this is the individual whiteboard (often used in literacy lessons). Children can either work with you or their talk partner to draft and redraft sentences using their individual whiteboards. Once they (and you) are satisfied with the sentence, they can copy it into their book.

Universal issues in writing in science

Science, like many other subjects on the curriculum, raises a number of issues in relation to children writing in science.

- Children write long rambling sentences – Help children by encouraging them to break down their ideas and experiences into smaller chunks. Show them photographs of what they did and challenge them to put the photographs in order and write a sentence about each one. You could also tell children that they have three bullet points to describe what they did and then support them in writing a sentence for each bullet point.
- Children do not write what the teacher or teaching assistant wants them to write – Guide children into thinking about what is appropriate. You might ask them to think about what are the most important things to write about and list them, then help children to write a sentence about each item in their list.
- Children do not use scientific language in their writing – Tell children which words you expect them to use; give children a list of words (not too many) and tell them to use use each word once in their piece of work.

Children can often give up on writing something after only a few lines, saying that they don't know what to write. They may find writing difficult and be unable to sustain long pieces of writing because they lack confidence in what they know or their own writing skills and will not commit pen to paper. They may be unable to conceive the whole thing and can only think of bits.

They may have difficulty with their short-term memory or trouble sequencing events.

Think of ways that children can communicate by using less writing. Have them:

- write a set of bullet points;
- use strip cartoons (the children draw pictures and write a sentence under each one);
- draw labelled diagrams;
- share one piece of writing for a group (the children could take turns being the responsible writer).

Using science writing frames

Many teachers use a science writing frame to support children when they are planning an investigation or recording what they have done. These are very useful but might not be appropriate for the children you support. The children might not be able to read them, the framework may be too complex or demand too much writing.

If this is the case, you should discuss the use of writing frames with the teacher and decide on appropriate alternatives. (You may already have created some yourself.) Figure 6.2 shows two frameworks: one relies on the children to complete everything; the other is an alternative, it allows the children to use different ways to communicate what they have done, which requires less writing.

Describe, explain, prediction, hypothesis

The majority of children find it difficult to write descriptions, explanations or conclusions. In fact many teachers find that they themselves are unsure about what the differences between each of these is in relation to science. If adults find the concepts difficult it is not surprising that children do as well.

My investigation	Which sugar dissolves the fastest?
The question _____	I used: <u>Beaker</u>, thermometer, ruler, <u>water</u>, oil, <u>sugar</u>, salt, <u>spoon</u>
What I used _____	The _____ sugar dissolves the fastest. It dissolved in _____ seconds.
What I did _____	**A picture of what I did**
My results _____	
My conclusion _____	
What I would change _____	

Figure 6.2 Standard and alternative writing frames

Here's a quick review of the words:

- To describe is *to say or tell* what happened or what something looks like or does.

- To explain is to say or tell *why* something happened or looks the way it does or does what it does. The word 'because' moves a statement from a description to an explanation.

- To predict is to say what you *think will happen* but not to explain why you think that. Very young children will not predict; they will just guess because they have not enough scientific knowledge to use, or experience to draw upon.

- To hypothesise is to *offer a reason* for your prediction. A hypothesis follows a prediction and again, the word 'because' moves the prediction on.

Figure 6.3 Examples of a description and explanation: sugar dissolving in water

Figure 6.4 Examples of a prediction and hypothesis: the properties of plastic

Be a good role model and make language in science fun

Try to make learning scientific language and writing in science fun, so that children are motivated to learn and look forward to writing in science and have success in their writing. Break down tasks into smaller more manageable parts and always praise children for even the smallest accomplishment. You can play games such as bingo, hangman, dominoes, what's in the box, snap, hot seating, 20 questions, splat!, word search. Make sure that you remind children of the strategies that they use in literacy to learn words and write, and make sure that you are a good role model. You should always use the correct scientific language and help to reinforce and consolidate their understanding of words.

When supporting children in writing about their science, make sure that you:

- help them sequence events;

- move them from giving descriptions to explanations;

- challenge them to use words appropriately.

You can help make writing in science interesting, challenging and at the right level for the child. If you do, you will be effective in helping children move forward in their science.

To check that you are prepared to support the use of language in a science lesson, ask yourself:

- Do I know the scientific vocabulary the children need to learn and some of the difficulties children might have with individual words?

- Do I know and use a range of approaches for learning new scientific words?

- Do I know a range of strategies for encouraging children to write in science?

- Do I assess how useful writing frames are and change them according to the needs of individuals?

- Am I confident that I know what the words mean and can help children to understand them?

- Do I play word games?

- Am I a good role model and do I make learning scientific words fun?

REMEMBER

- Language is central to science.

- Science has a specific language and ways of writing that we need to help children develop.

- Children will learn scientific words more easily if lessons are exciting and fun.

- There are many creative ways to support children in using scientific language.

CHAPTER 7

Recording and communicating

In this chapter we will explore:

- the challenges of supporting recording and communication in science;
- different approaches to recording and communication in science;
- planning to support recording and communication.

The challenges of supporting recording and communication in science

Teaching assistants are increasingly being required to take more of a lead when supporting children in the classroom. This support might include making decisions about the best way for children to record and communicate their science. Quite often teaching assistants will be supporting children who have difficulties with writing and are easily frustrated when asked to write about their science. Sometimes it is because they know what to say but can't write it or they find it difficult to explain things.

Writing in science can be difficult for some children; they might struggle with some or all of the following:

- spelling;
- grammar;
- creating a sentence;
- writing explanations;
- not knowing what to write about;
- using scientific language.

Children need to develop their writing and communication skills in this area of the curriculum, but this must not get in the way of their learning in science. The important questions in relation to recording and communication in a science lesson are:

- What are our learning objectives?
- Is this a science lesson or is it a literacy lesson?

When supporting children in a science lesson the priorities are science knowledge and skills. If writing in science frustrates children and puts them in danger of not learning in science – or indeed enjoying it – then we have to think of appropriate alternatives. This does not mean that children do not need to write in science, but that we need to support them and help them succeed.

Some children excel in writing about science, indeed some of the more able should be expected to use many different approaches in communicating their science and match these to specific audiences. If you are supporting such children then your role will be to challenge children to:

- be concise;

- explain their ideas;

- use and correctly spell appropriate scientific language;

- organise recording and communication;

- be aware of the needs of the given audience;

- choose and use different ways of communicating their science.

Different approaches to recording and communicating in science

Children can record and communicate their science in many ways (see below). Not every approach will be used in any one year group, but during a child's time in primary school all of them should be experienced. There are too many approaches to discuss each one in detail. In the next sections I discuss some of the more essential approaches.

- advertisements
- banners
- biographical and autobiographical writing
- brainstorms
- bullet points
- captions
- cartoons
- circuit diagrams
- collages
- concept cartoons
- concept maps
- consumer information
- dance
- diagrams
- dictionaries
- display
- drama
- emails
- faxes
- flow charts
- glossaries
- graphs
- instructions
- interviews
- labels
- leaflets
- letters
- lists
- models
- newspaper articles
- note-taking
- observational sketches and drawings

- paintings
- photographs
- poems
- posters
- prose
- questions
- reports
- role-play
- science-fiction stories
- scribed sentences and words

- sequenced pictures
- sequenced sentences
- shadow puppets
- songs
- stories
- tables
- talk and talk partners
- tape recording
- text messages
- video

SOMETHING TO THINK ABOUT

Look at the bulleted list of ways to record and communicate. Which of the approaches have you seen used in a science lesson? Choose two approaches you have not used but think might be useful and interesting. Talk with your teacher about trying them out, explaining why you think they are appropriate. Afterwards, make sure you reflect on how successful the approaches were.

Tables

Tables are an essential part of science and an important way of recording information and communicating it to someone else. Tables allow us to show information, usually data, in a clear and concise way. Figure 7.1 shows a typical table.

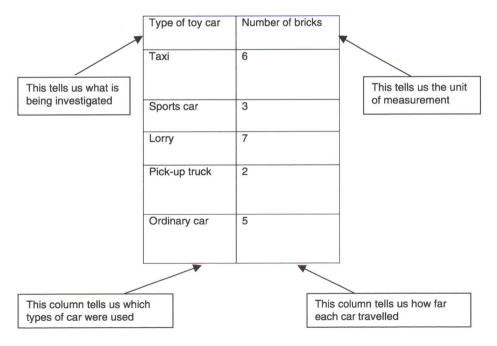

Figure 7.1 Which toy car goes the furthest?

If the children complete the table themselves, we know that they understand what a table is and how to use it. If we want to know if they understand the data in a table, we need to ask them questions, for example:

- *Which car went the furthest?*
- *Which car went three bricks?*
- *How far did the taxi go?*
- *Which car would you choose to ride in? Why?*

Graphs

There are different types of graph in science. Graphs help children organise data so that it is easy to read; they can see how something changes as well as patterns and relationships.

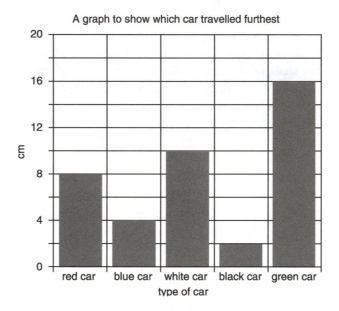

Figure 7.2 A bar graph

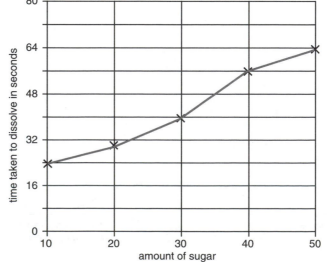

Figure 7.3 A line graph

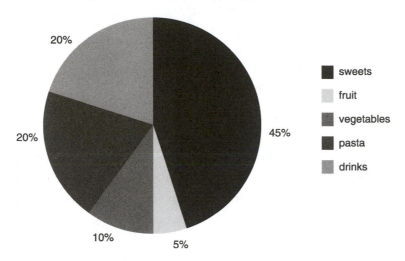

A pie chart to show percentage of types of food eaten

- sweets
- fruit
- vegetables
- pasta
- drinks

20%

20%

45%

10%

5%

Figure 7.4 A pie chart

When drawing graphs children must learn to label the graph with:

- The X axis, known as the horizontal axis. In a fair test investigation the X axis is what has been changed. (You can get the children to remember this by having them lie flat on the floor with arms and legs forming an X shape.)

- The Y axis, known as the vertical axis. In a fair test investigation the Y axis is what the children have measured. (You can get the children to remember this by having them stand up straight with their arms up in the air in a Y shape.)

- A scale on each axis.

Bar charts are used throughout primary school. Older primary children need to know when to choose a bar chart and a line graph. A simple rule of thumb is:

- if the X axis is words and the Y axis is numbers then it is a bar chart;

- if the X axis is numbers and the Y axis is numbers then it is a line chart.

Pie charts show data by comparing parts of a whole. For example, a pie chart about the way you spend your time at home will show pie slices of different sizes for the amount of time you spend on activities such as watching television, gardening, cleaning and so on. The whole pie is all your time at home. The size of the slice can be stated as either a fraction or percentage.

Venn diagrams and sets

Children do not need to communicate what they know using written language. For example, when they are sorting (classifying) things, they could record their ideas by putting objects in hoops or large paper circles, on sections of a large piece of paper or in different trays or containers.

When children are sorting, you might ask them questions about why they put objects in different places, for example:

- *Why did you put that there?*
- *What else could you put in that section?*
- *Can any objects go in two different sections?*

Labels

Labels are a good way of showing different parts of things such as plants or animals. You could make a set of labels (laminated labels with Velcro on the back, for sticking on felt boards, for instance). When you are using labels, make sure the children can:

- say the word;
- explain the word;
- spell the word;
- explain why it belongs where they are placing it.

To differentiate writing ability you could make the labels:

- blank, for children to mark make or write their own word;
- with a picture and word, for children to attach it to the object;
- with a word only.

Captions

A caption is an explanation on a label, a small piece of information, usually not more that one or two sentences long. When children write a caption they might be working from memory or they might be rewriting information that they have read in a book or on the internet. Children might find it easier to write captions by drafting and redrafting using small individual whiteboards. You can support them to:

- use appropriate scientific vocabulary;
- write phrases or sentences that are short and concise;
- use their subject knowledge;
- research information;
- be accurate.

Models

Children make all sorts of models in science. In electricity, children might make a working model of a lighthouse, a car, or a house and they could place a label with a caption next to their model. The caption might explain how they made their model, how to use it or even show a circuit diagram. Older children might make a model of the digestive system and use captions to explain the function of different parts of the system.

Photographs

Photographs are excellent ways of recording what has happened in science. Now that schools have digital cameras we can click, save and print whenever we want to, or rather when the children want to. Children should decide what to photograph and then take the pictures themselves, not the teacher or the teaching assistant. Don't forget the 'hands-off' rule; this will help children develop their abilities to use ICT across the curriculum. Here are some good times for taking photographs:

- To record changes in the environment. Children could take photographs throughout the school year and place them in a 'Big Book' showing different aspects of environmental change.

- To record working in the water tray or role-play area. Encourage children to take photographs of themselves and friends working in these areas so that they can show and tell others about what they have done and found out.

- To record changes due to cooking. Take photographs of the different parts of the cooking process. Use them with children and ask them to explain what happened and what caused the changes, whether the changes are reversible or irreversible, and to put them in order and explain what happened next.

Annotated digital photographs

Children can take digital photographs of:

- a model they have made;

- something they have measured;

- a series of changes in something (for example, popcorn before and after it has popped).

Children should learn to become independent in using the digital camera and be given regular opportunities to take their own photographs. However, there will be times when the teaching assistant could use a digital camera to record what the children are doing. When printed the picture could then be used:

- to put into a Big Book to record what children have been doing;

- to annotate with children's comments and ideas before placing it as part of a display or in their workbook;

- as a focus for discussion;

- so that the children can sequence events, placing the pictures in order, for example, a bean seed growing into a flowering plant.

Strip cartoons

Strip cartoons are pictures with captions. The teaching assistant can decide how many pictures the children should use by folding the paper into two, four, six or more parts. For example, if the children were asked to create a set of pictures about how they found out which magnet was the strongest, your role would be to challenge the children to think about:

- the most important things to put in the pictures;
- the picture that needs to come first, and which should follow it;
- what should go into the last picture (and why).

Pictures and sentences

Some children will benefit from drawing a picture, then explaining to the teaching assistant and writing an explanatory sentence underneath it. You might then help children to:

- construct and write a sentence (using their individual whiteboard to draft the sentence);
- construct a sentence (you could write it on the whiteboard for redrafting before writing it beside the picture).

One of the disadvantages of children drawing pictures is that it is time-consuming and leaves little time to discuss the picture and get on with what the children know in science.

Instructions

Having children write a set of instructions can be helpful for those children who find writing difficult, particularly prose or sequences of events. Teachers sometimes ask children to write the instructions for a child in a younger year group. Instructions might be pictorial or short, numbered sentences. When children are writing instructions, you can:

- ask them to show you what to do, step by step, having them construct a sentence after each step;
- take photographs of children engaged in the activity and ask them to put the photographs in order. You can use the same photographs as reminders to the children of what they did in the activity;
- have children in another group read the first group's instructions and try to follow them; this will show the children that writing in science has a real purpose.

Diagrams

Diagrams show information concisely. Diagrams must have:

- a title;
- arrows that point to labels or captions (they are usually drawn with a ruler).

Children might draw diagrams of anything but they commonly draw diagrams of:

- how they set up equipment in an investigation;
- the human body;

- the digestive system;
- the parts of a plant;
- how we see things.

Letters

Some teachers like to use an interesting starting point for science: they arrange for a letter to be sent to their class that contains a question to answer or a problem to solve. When the children have finished their activity, they reply to the letter explaining what they have done and found out.

A good example is a letter from 'Teddy', who has lost his raincoat and needs a new one. Teddy asks the children to find out which material would be best for his new raincoat. After they have tested different materials to find out which is waterproof, they write back to Teddy.

Children really enjoy responding to a letter. Not only is it an interesting way to communicate their science, but they also learn the literacy skill of writing letters.

Videos

Surprisingly even the youngest children in a school can use a video camera. Video suits children who have writing difficulties as well as those who are more able. Some children who find writing frustrating become articulate when using a camera to explain what they have done and know. For children who are more able, the challenge is to create a commentary that is clear, concise, conveys scientific understanding and uses scientific vocabulary. Children could film their partners working; older children could decide which parts of an investigation they want to film and provide a running commentary to what is happening.

If you are supporting children who are using a video camera, step back, watch and listen. Don't expect perfection, do make suggestions and encourage children to play back extracts and decide whether they want to film parts again with different dialogue.

Poems

Poems are not just for English! They can be great starting points in science. Here are some simple frameworks that can be used.

Imagine you have been looking at caterpillars with children in the classroom. You have discussed what they look like, how they move, where they live, what they eat and so on.

Children create a poem simply by answering questions with words or phrases (see Figure 7.5). Children are very impressed with their own efforts and that of their friends when they are shared.

Planning to support recording and communication

The next time you support children in a science lesson, talk with the teacher about the different ways of recording and communicating in science.

Science questions	A poem
What am I?	A caterpillar
What colour am I?	Green like a lettuce
What shape am I?	Long like a tube
Where do I live?	Living on nettles
How do I move?	Crawling, stretching and squashing
What do I remind you of?	Like a concertina

Figure 7.5 Science questions and a poem

Ask yourself and the teacher the following questions:

- Do the children need to write in this lesson?

- If they do need to record, which is the best way for the children?

- Could we just talk about the activities?

- How can I help the children to be more precise, concise, use their scientific knowledge and scientific language to communicate what they know and have been doing in science?

Do not be afraid to share the list of alternative ways to record and communicate with your teacher.

To make sure you are supporting recording and communication, ask yourself:

- What difficulties do my children have in writing about science? Why? What can I do to help them?

- Do I understand the different kinds of graphs, what the children have to know about them and how they use them?

- How many different ways of recording and communicating have I used in science?

- What new ways would be appropriate to use with my children?

- Can I get children to write poems in science?

- Have I talked to the teacher about the different ways the children could record and communicate?

REMEMBER

- There are many different ways for children to record and communicate what they think and what they do in science.

- Your role is to choose the most appropriate way for children to record and communicate their science depending on their individual needs.

- Transfer strategies from literacy into science to support children in improving their recording and communication.

Using equipment and resources

In this chapter we will explore:

- developing children's independence in using science equipment;
- ensuring health and safety in science;
- key science equipment.

Developing children's independence in using science equipment

The science curriculum demands that children should:

- learn to use scientific equipment;
- know when it is appropriate to use different types of scientific equipment;
- know how to use equipment safely and with respect;
- be able to choose the equipment they need from a range of items;
- be able to organise themselves to find the equipment that they need;
- be able to use alternatives or improvise where they do not have the equipment that they need.

The key phrase is 'children should', which means that children, not the teacher or teaching assistant, are the decision-makers when choosing and using equipment. They may need support in developing this independence and here the role of the teaching assistant is crucial.

Helping children make their own decisions about scientific equipment

When you are helping children make their own decisions about scientific equipment, remember that not all approaches will work first time. Children need adults who are working with them to be consistent in their approaches. They also need to be challenged to have confidence in choosing and using equipment.

Here are some ways you can help:

1   Put out equipment for children to choose from (don't just give them the equipment).

2   Make choices obvious (depending on the age of the children). For example, if very young children are measuring liquid, ask them what kind of measuring tool is right. Show them things such as a measuring cup, a tape measure, a clock. The choice will be obvious (and perhaps get a laugh!), but they will become confident immediately in their ability to choose the right equipment.

3   Make the choice progressively more sophisticated. In the above example, once the children have confidently chosen a container for liquid, ask them what kind: a watering can, a bucket, a tiny beaker, a bigger beaker. Ask them to explain why each item is appropriate (or not!). Ask children who have chosen the right container to choose between containers that measure in different units, for example teaspoons or cups (non-standard) and litres and millilitres (standard). This also gives you a chance to start talking about volumes rather than amounts – and to use the correct scientific vocabulary.

Remember to respect children's decisions; sometimes they see novel ways of using equipment. Before you redirect them, check their reasons for their choice. Also, let the children handle the equipment; they should be given the opportunity and responsibility to get equipment out and put it away.

SOMETHING TO THINK ABOUT

How can you help children make their own decisions about which equipment to use and how and when to use it?

Think about these questions:

- What strategies have you seen teachers use to promote independence?

- What kind of approaches do you already use with children in science?

- What other ways could you use?

Make a list of your ideas; you might like to share your list with your teacher or other teaching assistants. You could also try some of the approaches suggested in this section.

Ensuring health and safety

The ASE book *Be Safe!* (2001) provides guidelines to teachers in primary schools on how to ensure children are safe when engaged in science.

When supporting children in science, particularly during practical work, there are a number of things that you should think about.

- First, who is responsible for the safety of the children? Both teachers and teaching assistants are in fact responsible for the children in their care. It is therefore important that everyone is familiar with the school's science health and safety policy. If you do not know what the policy is, ask for a copy to read. All schools should have an up-to-date copy of *Be Safe!*. Be sure to read the sections that relate to the science you are supporting.

- Second, do the children have a role in health and safety in science? They do. Children should be taught to recognise hazards in science and assess the risk to themselves and others. They also need to learn how to handle science hazards safely. It is our job to make sure that children are safe, not to sanitise science to the point that children do not face risks and consequently do not learn how to behave responsibly.

Wherever possible you should use positive approaches to health and safety by modeling good practice as well as encouraging children to think through health and safety issues and suggest their own solutions. One way to do this is to ask 'What do we need to do to be safe?'

A safe working environment

Making sure that the classroom is a safe working environment is usually a matter of common sense, for example, if children are using water, ensure that they are working:

- near a sink to avoid trailing water across the classroom;
- on a table top so spills can be mopped up;
- where there are appropriate floor tiles;
- and that there are paper towels for clearing spilled water.

In science children often use resources that require children to follow basic hygiene rules. A useful way of encouraging children to take responsibility for their own welfare is to ask them to create their own set of rules to follow. For example, when cooking in science you could ask the children to think about how they should behave so that they are safe and hygienic and then make a poster to show their rules and remind them that they had agreed to:

- tie hair back
- remove or tie back any loose clothing
- wash hands
- avoid touching their hair and face
- avoid sneezing or coughing over food
- not to use the cooker unsupervised
- mop up any spills
- wash and put away all equipment.

It is your responsibility to make sure that any equipment you use with the children you are supporting is appropriate and safe. This ranges from ensuring that if children are carrying equipment around the classroom or school it is safely packed and not too heavy for them to carry, to ensuring that no items are broken and potentially dangerous, such as thermometers.

Remember, if in doubt – ask. Better to be safe than sorry.

Key science equipment

The following provides brief reviews of key science equipment used in primary school and their health and safety features. It is the role of the teaching assistant to familiarise themselves with science equipment used in the classroom and to become confident in its use.

Candles

If supervised by an adult, older children can use candles, or preferably 'night-lights', to burn small samples of materials (including fabrics), heat liquid and melt substances such as butter, chocolate and cheese. Night-lights are small, safe candles in a foil container; they should be placed in a tray or bowl of sand so that they cannot be knocked over and the sand can be used to put them out. Ensure that children act responsibly and ask them to check that they do not have loose hair or clothing that could catch fire.

Clocks and stopwatches

Be careful which timing devices are used by children; stopwatches might be great fun but often children cannot manage to read or understand the decimal place. You could cover over this part of the stopwatch so that children only deal with the whole seconds if that is appropriate. You might need to teach children how to use a stop-clock or a stopwatch. They can be quite complex with a number of buttons. Allow children time to 'explore' them before they have to use them to time something in an activity. Always check that children understand how to use them.

Data loggers

Don't be put off by the technical name, a data logger is a piece of ICT equipment that can take and store different kinds of measurements including temperature, light, sound, pulse rate, pH, motion (how far something tilts) and how fast something moves (light gate). These are usually very user-friendly packages with clear instructions and ideas for use in science activities. They are designed so that the children can set up the computer to do any of the following:

- take measurements;
- take measurements at regular intervals, e.g. every 2 seconds, every 5 minutes;
- take measurements for a set period of time, for example, for 10 minutes or overnight when the children are not in the classroom;
- show the measurements in a table;
- show the measurements presented as a graph.

Batteries and bulbs

Batteries come in all shapes and sizes and different schools use different types. The power of the battery is shown on the label in volts, e.g. 1.5V, 3V, 4.5V. A 1.5V is a single cell or battery; all the rest are multiples of 1.5V.

When using bulbs (lamps) make sure that the wattage on the bulb matches the voltage on the battery quite closely, otherwise a 4.5V battery could blow a 1.5 watt bulb.

Batteries should be stored so that the terminals (metal ends) do not touch – if they do, the batteries could overheat and short circuit.

Battery holders are usually used for round batteries so that a number of batteries can be put together to power components in a circuit.

Bulbs are also called lamps; they come in different sizes and should be matched to the right battery (see above). Inside the bulb is a fine piece of wire called a filament. When this breaks the bulb will not work.

Bulb holders come in different shapes and sizes but all allow a bulb to be held securely in position within a circuit. If a circuit does not work, check that the bulb is screwed in properly.

Buzzers

There are different types of buzzers that make different sounds, which of course children love to use.

Crocodile clips

Crocodile clips are the metal clips that clip onto parts of a circuit (most wire leads are ready-made leads with crocodile clips on the end).

LEDs (Light Emitting Diodes)

LEDs are indicator lights, for example, the light on your computer that indicates if the computer is on or off. An alternative to bulbs, they are usually coloured and used in models.

Switch

There are many types of switches, from the humble push switch to toggle switches, knife switches and reed switches, which use a magnet to turn components in a circuit on and off.

Motors

Motors are great fun because they allow things to move in a circuit, for example, for wheels to go round, a propeller to turn, and a clown's bow tie to spin.

Wires

Many schools have different kinds of wire for children to use. Most purchase crocodile clips with wire already attached, although older children might cut wire encased in plastic to the length they require. High resistance wire does not have the plastic sheath around it, it is 'bare wire' and is used for making dimmer switches and testing to find out if the length or thickness of wire affects the brightness of a bulb.

Force meters (Newton meter)

Force meters measure pull forces and come in different sizes (each size a different colour), according to how much pull force they can measure. Check that they start at zero and if not turn the small nut at the end to reset it.

Hand lenses

Children love using these but like many pieces of science equipment they do need to learn to use them properly and with care. Hand-held lenses require the user to move the lens away from and closer to the object under observation in order to focus and get a clear view. Children must learn not to mishandle these as some scratch or crack easily.

Magnets

Magnets come in all shapes and sizes including horseshoe magnets, magnetic wands, magnetic balls and even magnetic strips that are like thin plastic sheets. Sometimes the smaller magnets are stronger than the larger magnets, while some, like 'floating magnets', can be made to float above each other. Things to know and remember about this resource are, first, that a magnet's magnetism can be destroyed if it is not handled carefully. Do not allow children to bang them or drop them frequently. Also, remember that if children use iron filings then those must be in container with a lid because the fine iron filings can be breathed in and this is a health hazard. Magnets should not be placed near computers, watches or credit cards.

Microscopes

There are two main types of microscopes used in schools:

1   Binocular microscopes, which are simple to use. Children put the object to view on the viewing platform and use the focus wheel to bring the object into clear view.

2   Digital microscope – this is connected to a computer and allows children to view objects on a computer screen. This is a great piece of ICT equipment that provides awesome views of everyday objects. It also allows children to record still images, video clips and to change images. Children find them both easy to use and fascinating.

Mirrors

Glass mirrors can be used in the classroom, and should be used in some circumstances because they provide a better reflection than plastic mirrors. Glass mirrors should be backed with tape or sticky-backed plastic so that if the mirror is dropped the pieces stay together (see *Be Safe!* for further information). There are different kinds of mirrors, some called convex (bow outwards), others concave (cave inwards). When children look in such mirrors their image is quite different from a normal mirror. These kind of mirrors are often used in a Hall of Mirrors at fairgrounds. There are also flexible mirrors, which can be bent to produce special effects.

Push meter

Push meters measure a push force, for example, how much of a push force it takes to make something move. Some push meters look like Pull Meters (Newton meters) and the scale for measuring is in Newtons.

Syringes

Syringes are often used in water play with early years but they can also be used to make hydraulic and pneumatic systems (where water or air is placed in tubing and a syringe at one end is depressed and the water or air in the system pushes the syringe at the other end out). They are also really useful for measuring small amounts of water and are often used to measure water when growing seeds and plants.

Thermometers

There is a wide range of thermometers available for children to use. They are used for different purposes, for example, spirit thermometers are used when children take the temperature of water, while forehead thermometers are often used in early years to help children to understand ideas about body temperature. Here are some things to remember about thermometers:

- mercury thermometers are not used in primary schools because the mercury is dangerous;

- spirit thermometers must be handled with care; they can and do break easily;

- when holding a spirit thermometer make sure you do not hold the bulb or any part where the coloured liquid is because this can affect the reading;

- thermometers with a scale are difficult for many children to use because they might not understand the idea of scale or it might be too small and difficult to read;

- electronic thermometers are often easier for even the very young children to use and read.

SOMETHING TO THINK ABOUT

When supporting children in science lessons have you come across any equipment that you are unsure about, perhaps in how to use it or the safety implications? Make a list. If any of the items on your list have not been discussed in this chapter, ask your teacher or the science coordinator to go over the purpose, use and safe care of the items.

To check your awareness of health and safety, ask yourself the following questions:

- Do I know where equipment is stored in the classroom and school? Do I always check that I have the equipment needed for the lesson before it starts?

- What approaches do I use to support children becoming independent in using science equipment? What other approaches could I try?

- Do I understand the health and safety issues related to the equipment the children are using? How will I check my knowledge?

- Do I have a copy of the ASE *Be Safe!* book?

Do you need to learn about some items of equipment? Find time to ask someone about them.

Remember that working with children in science requires you to be patient with children who do not know how to use equipment, are unsure what to use and need practice to be able to use the equipment with confidence. It also requires you to be firm with yourself about not making choices for children and making sure that they, not you, use the equipment, no matter how long this takes! Patience is a virtue.

REMEMBER

- The science curriculum demands that children are able to choose and use equipment. Children must be able to develop the ability to be responsible.

- You must resist doing things for children, unless they are physically unable to manage.

- Teachers have to assess children's ability to choose and use science equipment appropriately and safely.

Bibliography

ASE (2001) *Be Safe! Health and safety in primary school science and technology*, 3rd edn. Hatfield: Associaton for Science Education.

Edwards, S. (2004) *Helping Hands: Supporting Writing.* London: David Fulton Publisher.

Feasey, R. (1998) 'Effective Questioning in Science', in Sherrington, R. (ed.) *ASE Guide to Primary Science Education.* Cheltenham: Stanley Thornes.

Gray, C., Rodrigues, S., Simpson, L. and Sowdon, C. *Primary Science Date Handling Activities: Using graphs, tables and sensors.* Durham: University of Durham.

Harlen, W. (2006) *Teaching, Learning and Assessing Science 5 – 12*, 4th edn. London: Sage.

Keogh, B. and Naylor, S. (1996) *Starting Points for Science.* Cheshire: Millgate House Publications.

Phipps, R. (1997) 'Schemes of work in Primary Science', Evaluation and Research in Education, **11**(1), p. 22

Smith, C. (1998) 'Schemes of Work', in Sherrington, R. (ed.) *ASE Guide to Primary Science Education.* Cheltenham: Stanley Thornes.

Index

ALSO AVAILABLE IN THIS SERIES:

Primary Mathematics for Teaching Assistants

Sylvia Edwards

This easy-to-use and accessible book has been specifically written for teaching assistants. It is packed with practical activities, ideas and strategies to help you to enhance your pupils' numeracy and mathematics skills and build on your own subject knowledge. It:

- includes a cross-curricular focus that shows how to stop pupils forgetting fundamental skills when changing subjects

- suggests methods and ideas for assessment

- is written in line with the national strategies

- suggests activities for developing problem-solving and thinking skills

- includes a breakdown of mathematical principles.

Use this book whether you're studying for qualifications or just keen to support your pupils better.

ISBN: 978–1–84312–428–3

ALSO AVAILABLE IN THIS SERIES:

Primary ICT for Teaching Assistants

John Galloway

This easy-to-use and accessible book has been specifically written for teaching assistants. It is packed with practical activities, ideas and strategies to help you to enhance your pupils' competence in ICT. It:

- shows how you can support students within the ICT programme of study – even if you're not a confident ICT user yourself

- tackles tricky issues such as assessment and progression

- suggests activities for developing skills, familiarity and understanding

- provides ideas and advice for effective use of ICT in other subjects

- shows how ICT can be a really effective tool for inclusion.

Use this book whether you're studying for qualifications or just keen to support your pupils better.

ISBN: 978–1–84312–446–7